THE JUNCTIONS
OF TIME

Pastor Mark Amoateng, MD

Pastor Mark Amoateng, MD

DEDICATION

I dedicate this book to my *'Trailblazers'*. Your passion, love and zeal for God is unparalleled. By your God, scale heights and by your God, run through a troop.

Pastor Mark Amoateng, MD

CONTENTS

ACKNOWLEDGMENTS

I will like to express my gratitude to you **Prophetess Sheryl Hill** for all your help and the administrative work you do for Christ Palace International Ministries. Thank you for your assistance in editing and proofreading this book.

Special thanks also go to **Patience Djarbeng** for her time in editing and proofreading this piece.

INTRODUCTION

"Therefore my people are gone into captivity, because [they have] no knowledge: and their honorable men [are] famished, and their multitude dried up with thirst" (Isaiah 5:13 KJV)

The value of knowledge cannot be overestimated. Accurate knowledge, right knowledge and adequate knowledge is paramount if you must make your mark on the earth. Most people find themselves locked up, limited and frustrated because they lack adequate knowledge. I believe everybody knows something. But whether what you know is enough to make you operate as a master in life is another question altogether.

The knowledge of time is very crucial for your existence on earth. This is because everything that happens on the earth happens in time. The bible declares there is a time for everything.

"To every [thing there is] a season, and a time to every purpose under the heaven: A time to be born, and a time to die; a time to plant, and a time to pluck up [that which is] planted; (Ecclesiastes 3:1-2 KJV)

You must know the spirituality of time. God is a Spirit and so whatever comes from Him has a spirituality attached to it. God created time. Time has spirituality attached to it and when you know this and take advantage of it, you will be in charge.

The scriptures speak of the men of Issachar that ruled and were in command because they had understanding of the times.

"And of the children of Issachar, [which were men] that had understanding of the times, to know what Israel ought to do; the heads of them [were] two hundred; and all their brethren [were] at their commandment" (1 Chronicles 12:32 KJV)

Time is a neutralizer. Everybody has the same amount. The poor and the rich have this in common; they have the same amount of time. Time and chance happen to all men.

"I returned, and saw under the sun, that the race [is] not to the swift, nor the battle to the strong, neither yet bread to the wise, nor yet riches to men of understanding, nor yet favour to men of skill; but time and chance happeneth to them all" (Ecclesiastes 9:11 KJV)

In this book we seek to explore what is called the Junctions of Time. You will get to know how to use time to your advantage. You will also discover what spiritual portals are and how to also create them.

Its exploration will be based wholly on the Word of God. The word of God is supreme and superior. It has the final say on all matters of life. Get set and ready for an explosive revelation from the Spirit of God.

CHAPTER 1

ETERNITY AND TIME

"For thus saith the high and lofty One that inhabiteth eternity, whose name [is] Holy;" (Isaiah 57:15 KJV).

There is a dwelling place for every creature. Jesus declared, *"Foxes have holes, and birds of the air [have] nests;" (Luke 9:58 KJV).* But where and what is the dwelling place of God, the creator of everyone and everything? The Prophet Isaiah by divine insight revealed to us the habitation of God. God dwells in Eternity. God lodges and inhabits eternity. What is eternity and where is this eternity?

Eternity is a dimension where there is no beginning and no end. Eternity is an infinite, endless zone where the past is never past and the future is already present.

You must understand that God created one universe with two dimensions or realms. These two realms are:

1. The Spiritual realm or Unseen realm or Eternal realm or Eternity.

2. The Physical realm or the Seen Realm or the Earthly realm or Time.

So actually, God created a two-dimensional universe which is Eternity and Time. But He dwells in Eternity. In this Eternity or the spiritual realm there is no distance or time. There is no past, present or future in this realm.

Actually, the past, present and future are fused as one timeless dimension. This eternal realm is just an ever-present now. It is called the 'Nowness' of Eternity. It is always 'Now' in this zone.

In the time realm or dimension, there is past, present and future. There are boundaries. But not in the eternal realm. There are no boundaries or limitations.

God lives in this realm and He has no beginning of days nor end of life. There is no succession of moments in God's existence. That is why He is called I AM. He always Is. To have succession of moments means one event succeeds another. But God just happens. He doesn't have to wait for one event to be completed before He begins another. In this dimension God is always constant and consistent, never changing.

God dwells in eternity but He produced and gave to man what is called time. God has placed humanity in the time zone. And one day when we exit this zone we will dwell with God in eternity.

That being said, the eternal realm is the abode of spirits. So, because man has a part of Him which is spiritual, he can participate and interact with God who lives in the spirit realm. With your body which is your physical part, you relate to the physical realm or time zone. And with your spirit you function in the eternal realm.

Paul, the Apostle revealed the composition of man to the Thessalonians:

"And the very God of peace sanctify you wholly; and [I pray God] your whole spirit and soul and body be preserved blameless unto the coming of our Lord Jesus Christ" (1 Thessalonians 5:23 KJV).

THE DIFFERENCE BETWEEN THE EARTHLY TIME ZONE AND THE ETERNAL ZONE

Actually, you want to understand that everything takes place in the eternal realm where God lives or abides. Then whatever happens in the eternal realm is transported to this dimension called the time zone. So, the time zone as we have it is only a venue. Time is a zone which receives all the stuff which takes place in the eternal realm of God.

For example, your house is a venue which receives you. When you leave for work you leave the venue of your home. After work, you may buy some stuff from the mall. You may buy a smartphone for example. When you get back to your house, the smartphone too arrives at your home. What has happened to the smartphone is that it has changed venues. The smartphone was at the mall but now it has arrived at your house. It has changed addresses.

In the same vein, time is a venue which receives the stuff or creations or orchestrations that happen in the eternal realm where God lives. To receive anything from God, you must understand that the gifts and the events you desire of Him are located in the spiritual realm and must be transported into the physical realm. If you are believing God for healing, you must understand and know that the healing is in the eternal realm and must be transported into the time zone.

The next thing you want to understand about time is that, time is a gift God gave to man. The reason God gave time as a gift to man is so that man can experience God in time. We can experience the Eternal One in time. All the physical things God created and put in the time zone are to reveal to us the invisible qualities of God who inhabits eternity. *"For since the creation of the world God's invisible qualities-- his eternal power and divine nature-- have been clearly seen, being understood from what has been made, so that men are without excuse" (Romans 1:20 NIV).*

The mountains, the hills, the valleys, the seas and all creation prove the existence of a mighty God and by that you get to experience the magnificence of this mighty Personality called God. Even the starry heavens talk about God.

"The heavens declare the glory of God; and the firmament sheweth his handywork" (Psalms 19:1 KJV).

God therefore displays His great qualities and attributes in time so man can relate to the Eternal One.

TIME IS VERY IMPORTANT IF YOU LIVE ON THE EARTH

Beloved you must understand that if you live on the earth, time is very significant. Everything on this planet happens in time. *"To every [thing there is] a season, and a time to every purpose under the heaven" (Ecclesiastes 3:1 KJV).*
There is a time for everything which goes on under the sun. The Bible in Basic English renders this same verse this way:

"For everything there is a fixed time, and a time for every business under the sun" (Ecclesiastes 3:1 BBE).

As long as you live under the sun you must operate and understand the dynamics of time. When you live above the sun, time is not significant, but under the sun time is crucial. I am sure you know your body is living under the sun.

The writer of Ecclesiastes goes ahead to list for us all the purposes that go on under the sun in the succeeding verses of the same chapter.

"A time to be born, and a time to die; a time to plant, and a time to pluck up [that which is] planted; A time to kill, and a time to heal; a time to break down, and a time to build up; A time to weep, and a time to laugh; a time to mourn, and a time to dance; A time to cast away stones, and a time to gather stones together; a time to embrace, and a time to refrain from embracing; A time to get, and a time to lose; a time to keep, and a time to cast away;

7

A time to rend, and a time to sew; a time to keep silence, and a time to speak; A time to love, and a time to hate; a time of war, and a time of peace" *(Ecclesiastes 3:2-8 KJV).*

Things under the sun are done on the earth according to their season. There is a time for specific events to happen and manifest. In Psalms 102:13, God waited for a set time to favor Zion. Although God loved Zion, there was a time ordained for Zion to be favored. *"Thou shalt arise, [and] have mercy upon Zion: for the time to favour her, yea, the set time, is come" (Psalms 102:13 KJV).*

The beauty of life is seen when everything happens at its appointed time. When an event coincides with its appointed and ordained time its splendor and excellence is made manifest. *"He hath made every [thing] beautiful in his time:" (Ecclesiastes 3:11 KJV).*

Just imagine a 5- year old girl getting married. There is nothing beautiful about that because that is not the time for her to marry. But when she gets of age, the beauty of her marriage becomes ripe. Again, you never graduate the same day you matriculate in school. There is time for matriculation and there is a time for graduation. There is the chronology of events in time. And when things are done chronologically, wisdom and beauty are displayed.

FULLNESS OF TIME

The time appointed for an event to manifest in the physical realm is called the fullness of time. In Galatians 4:4, the blessed Apostle revealed Jesus could not come till the fullness of time arrived.

"But when the fulness of the time was come, God sent forth his Son, made of a woman, made under the law, To redeem them that were under the law, that we might receive the adoption of sons" (Galatians 4:4-5 KJV).

You see Adam and Eve sinned thousands of year ago in the garden of Eden. And God loved man so much that He wanted to redeem him by sending His son. But God's redemption plan could not manifest till the appointed time or the fullness of time.

Actually, God enacted the plan of redemption long time before it manifested in the zone or dimension called Time. Because the scriptures revealed to us that Jesus was crucified from the foundations of the earth.

"And all that dwell upon the earth shall worship him, whose names are not written in the book of life of the Lamb slain from <u>the foundation of the world</u>" (Revelation 13:8 KJV).

So actually, Jesus was crucified in the eternal realm, but the event which had already happened with respect to eternity was transported to the physical realm only at the appointed time. This was when the time was due. So in the maturation of time, events happen and manifest in the physical realm.

For example, there came a time when the Kingdom of God was at hand or a time when the Kingdom of God had come close to men. The kingdom existed in the eternal realm but till the maturation of time it could not manifest.

"The time has come," he said. "The kingdom of God is near. Repent and believe the good news!" (Mark 1:15 NIV).

Although there are appointed times for events to manifest, if we don't know and take advantage of it we can lose them or miss those divine appointments.

"And shall lay thee even with the ground, and thy children within thee; and they shall not leave in thee one stone upon another; because thou knewest not the time of thy visitation" (Luke 19:44 KJV).

When Jesus got to the city gates of Jerusalem He wept over it. And this was because they did not recognize the time of their visitation. The fullness of time for the visitation of Jerusalem had arrived, but they couldn't recognize it.

You must learn to be conscious of the timing and the seasons of God for your life so you don't miss the God ordained events of your life.

THOSE WHO TAKE ADVANTAGE OF TIME ARE IN COMMAND

Among the tribes of Israel, there was one tribe called Issachar. The scriptures revealed that all their brethren were at their command. They dictated what happened to their brethren. This was because they understood times and seasons.

"And of the children of Issachar, [which were men]

that had understanding of the times, to know what Israel ought to do; the heads of them [were] two hundred; and all their brethren [were] at their commandment" (I Chronicles 12:32 KJV).

The men of Issachar were in charge by reason of their understanding of time. By their understanding of time they knew exactly what to do at each time. Don't forget that it is by doing the right thing at the right time that brings the beauty of life.

You see in life, time happens to everyone. Everyone experiences the same number of hours in a day but those who take advantage of time and seasons stay in charge. And the way to take advantage of time is to have an accurate understanding of it.

"I returned, and saw under the sun, that the race [is] not to the swift, nor the battle to the strong, neither yet bread to the wise, nor yet riches to men of understanding, nor yet favour to men of skill; but time and chance happeneth to them all" (Ecclesiastes 9:11 KJV).

What matters under the sun is time. According to the preacher you can be swift and still lose a race. And you can be strong and lose a battle. You can be skillful and not enjoy favor. It is the understanding of time that is the most crucial and important factor of one's life.

Time and chance happens to all men. Nobody is disadvantaged with respect to time. Everyone has 24 hours in a day. The rich and the poor all have 24 hours in a day. The president and the peasant all have 24 hours in a day.

But the people that take advantage of time are the masters in life. It is not your color, beauty or skill which matters.

Time happens to everyone equally but as it happens to you, your understanding of time and you taking advantage of time will help you bring a lot of things from the eternal realm into the physical realm. The one who does not understand time will not know what to do with it to get what he or she wants. As a result, he watches it as it passes away.

So, in this book we seek to have a deeper understanding of time by turning our attention to an aspect of time call the "the Junctions of time" There are several aspects of time but our focus in this work is to have a greater grasp of the junctions of time.

CHAPTER 2

SPIRITUAL PORTALS

To have a clearer understanding of the Junctions of time you must first understand what is known as Spiritual portals. The word portal is simply defined as an opening or a doorway. It is an entrance, access point or a gateway. A portal is a communicating point between two places.

A Spiritual Portal is therefore any location, object, person or time zone that serves as a channel or medium or a window or a communicating point between the physical realm and the spiritual realm. They are entry points into the supernatural realm. Simply put, a spiritual portal is an entry point into the realm of the spirit.

A portal can be:
1. A place or a location
2. An object
3. A human personality can serve as an entry point into the realm of the spirit.
4. A Time zone.

Portals can also be classified as godly or they can be demonic. So, there are portals which are entry points for the demonic, and there are portals which are entry points for the godly or angelic.

The next thing you must understand about a portal, is that a portal is a place of increased spiritual activity and energy. And if a place has increased spiritual activity and energy, it means that there's an increase number of spirit beings. Portals serve as points of covenants with spiritual beings or spirit personalities.

If you are sensitive you can know and discern a portal when you get to one. When you meet an object, a location, a time zone, or a person who is a portal you will know if you are sensitive to the realm of the spirit.

LOCATION- PORTALS

I want to give examples of locations in the Bible which served as a Spiritual Portal. At such locations spiritual manifestations are easy and frequent. Spiritual activities like sacrifices and covenant are enacted.

WILDERNESS OF BEERSHEBA

Beersheba which is a city located in southern Israel is a portal. Let's examine the strange happenings that occurred at Beersheba.

Hagar had an Angelic Visitation

Hagar was the maidservant of Sarah. She was the mother of Ishmael. When Hagar and Ishmael were sent away from Abraham's house, they roamed through the desert till they got to the wilderness of Beersheba and an angel of God manifested to them.

"And Abraham rose up early in the morning, and took bread, and a bottle of water, and gave [it] unto Hagar, putting [it] on her shoulder, and the child, and sent her away: and she departed, and wandered in the wilderness of Beersheba. And the water was spent in the bottle, and she cast the child under one of the

shrubs. And she went, and sat her down over against [him] a good way off, as it were a bowshot: for she said, Let me not see the death of the child. And she sat over against [him], and lift up her voice, and wept. And God heard the voice of the lad; and the angel of God called to Hagar out of heaven, and said unto her, What aileth thee, Hagar? fear not; for God hath heard the voice of the lad where he [is]. Arise, lift up the lad, and hold him in thine hand; for I will make him a great nation" (Genesis 21:14-18 KJV).

There was a spiritual encounter or experience at the wilderness of Beersheba.

Abraham sacrificed and a covenant was enacted at Beersheba.

At Beersheba Abraham raised an altar and sacrificed. At the same place he also made a covenant with Abimelech. Actually, it was Abraham who named that place Beersheba because he made an oath with Abimelech. Beersheba means *Well of the Oath*. I believe the sacrifice and the covenant Abraham made in Beersheba created the spiritual portal.

"And Abraham took sheep and oxen, and gave them unto Abimelech; and both of them made a covenant. And Abraham set seven ewe lambs of the flock by themselves. And Abimelech said unto Abraham, What [mean] these seven ewe lambs which thou hast set by themselves? And he said, For [these] seven ewe lambs shalt thou take of my hand, that they may be a witness unto me, that I have digged this well. Wherefore he called that place Beersheba; because there they sware

both of them. Thus they made a covenant at Beersheba: then Abimelech rose up, and Phichol the chief captain of his host, and they returned into the land of the Philistines. And [Abraham] planted a grove in Beersheba, and called there on the name of the LORD, the everlasting God" (Genesis 21:27-33 KJV)

Isaac had an encounter at Beersheba

Isaac the son of Abraham roamed in the promised land. He had no spiritual encounters till one day he arrived at Beersheba. The same night he got to Beersheba, the Lord appeared to him. And God renewed the covenant He had with Abraham with Isaac. I believe God led Isaac to a spiritual portal so he could give him a spiritual experience.

"And he removed from thence, and digged another well; and for that they strove not: and he called the name of it Rehoboth; and he said, For now the LORD hath made room for us, and we shall be fruitful in the land. And he went up from thence to Beersheba. And the LORD appeared unto him the same night, and said, I [am] the God of Abraham thy father: fear not, for I [am] with thee, and will bless thee, and multiply thy seed for my servant Abraham's sake." (Genesis 26:22-24 KJV).

Jacob also had an encounter in the wilderness of Beersheba

Jacob the grandson of Abraham, and the son of Isaac also received an encounter with God in the wilderness of Beersheba. Between Beersheba and Haran was the wilderness of Beersheba. Jacob slept and at night he saw a ladder set up on the earth and the top reached towards heaven. And the angels of God were ascending and descending on it. And the Lord Himself stood above it. Why did this happen to Jacob? Because he had lighted at a Spiritual Portal.

"And Jacob went out from Beersheba, and went toward Haran. And he lighted upon a certain place, and tarried there all night, because the sun was set; and he took of the stones of that place, and put [them for] his pillows, and lay down in that place to sleep. And he dreamed, and behold a ladder set up on the earth, and the top of it reached to heaven: and behold the angels of God ascending and descending on it. And, behold, the LORD stood above it, and said, I [am] the LORD God of Abraham thy father, and the God of Isaac: the land whereon thou liest, to thee will I give it, and to thy seed;" (Genesis 28:10-13 KJV).

Jacob waited to sacrifice at Beersheba and had another encounter at Beersheba

Jacob again had another encounter at Beersheba. This time he was on his way to Egypt with all his family and possessions. His son Joseph was now the Prime Minister of Egypt. On his journey, he never offered a sacrifice till he got to Beersheba. I believe based on his prior experience he knew Beersheba was a spiritual portal because it was the place he saw the vision of the ladder reaching to heaven. And God manifested Himself to Jacob again at Beersheba.

"And Israel took his journey with all that he had, and came to Beersheba, and offered sacrifices unto the

God of his father Isaac. And God spake unto Israel in the visions of the night, and said, Jacob, Jacob. And he said, Here [am] I" (Genesis 46:1-2 KJV).

Elijah run to the wilderness of Beersheba when chased by Jezebel

Several years after the Patriarchs were no more, God raised a prophet in the land of Israel by the name of Elijah. There was a lot of idol worship in Israel at that time. And the most popular of the idols was Baal. Elijah gathered all the false prophets of Baal on Mount Carmel. And after displaying the power of God to the whole nation of Israel by commanding fire from heaven, he slayed all the prophets of Baal with the sword. When Jezebel, who was in charge of Baal worship, heard all that was done she was extremely angry and decided to kill Elijah, the Prophet. But Elijah ran away. Where did he go? He went to the wilderness of Beersheba. And right there an angel of the Lord touched him. Why did Elijah go to Beersheba? Elijah was a Prophet and I believe he knew there was a spiritual portal in the wilderness of Beersheba and the moment he got there he would have a divine encounter and be refreshed.

"And Ahab told Jezebel all that Elijah had done, and withal how he had slain all the prophets with the sword. Then Jezebel sent a messenger unto Elijah, saying, So let the gods do [to me], and more also, if I make not thy life as the life of one of them by tomorrow about this time. And when he saw [that], he arose, and went for his life, and came to Beersheba, which [belongeth] to Judah, and left his servant there. But he himself went a day's journey into the

wilderness, and came and sat down under a juniper tree: and he requested for himself that he might die; and said, It is enough; now, O LORD, take away my life; for I [am] not better than my fathers. And as he lay and slept under a juniper tree, behold, then an angel touched him, and said unto him, Arise [and] eat" (1 Kings 19:1-5 KJV).

JERUSALEM

One very important city is Jerusalem. The city of Jerusalem is a portal to the realm of the spirit. It is not just a tourist location. The reason people go for pilgrimage in Jerusalem is because, spiritually there is an opening into the heavenlies. There is increased spiritual activity in that city. This is as a result of the events and encounters which happened in the city years ago. Most worthy of note is the crucifixion, burial and resurrection of Our Lord Jesus Christ, the most important of all events for all time.

The temple of Solomon was also built in this city. The temple was a place of sacrifice and feasts of the Lord Most High. God literally dwelt there. And as a result, a portal to the spiritual was created.

It is not surprising the city has been the attention of the world for years.

OTHER EXAMPLES OF PLACES THAT CAN SERVE AS A LOCATION PORTAL

Church buildings are common examples of a location portal. Because of the spiritual activities of prayer, singing and giving of sacrifices, spiritual portals are created over a lot of church buildings. That is why a lot of miracles happen in church.

Certain Prayer mountains around the world. Prayer Mountains are places of intense prayers, meditation and fasting. An example is the Prayer Mountain in South Korea built by Rev. David Yonggi Cho, the pastor of the largest church in the world.

DEMONIC LOCATION PORTALS

One common place that serves as a demonic portal is a cemetery. This is why many occult practices take place there. Witchcraft initiations, voodoo initiations, fetishism, 'Juju' practices all take place there. It serves as an entry point to the demonic realm.

Other sites that can serve as portals are T- junctions, Traffic circles (roundabouts), and certain monuments especially those built with phallic designs. They serve as high energy points with high spiritual activities.

Also, sites of gruesome murder and terrible acts can serve as demonic location portals. Examples are homes and buildings where murders were conducted and witchcraft ceremonies occurred. They become what is commonly known as haunted houses.

Refuse dump sites also easily serve as demonic portals.

POINTS OF COVENANT

Spiritual portals also serve as what is known as points of covenants for demonic or satanic agents. These places are locations where satanic agents go to refresh their spiritual powers. It can be at the sea shores, certain water bodies, certain caves and evil forests. Such places are found all around the world with the western countries included.

In the book of Exodus, you will find Pharaoh going early in the morning to the river Nile. He was not just going there to bathe. He was a spiritual person. The Pharaohs of Egypt were not only kings but they were treated as gods also.

"Get thee unto Pharaoh in the morning; lo, he goeth out unto the water; and thou shalt stand by the river's brink against he come; and the rod which was turned to a serpent shalt thou take in thine hand" (Exodus 7:15 KJV)

The river served as a point of covenant to the demonic spirits he worshipped and the demonic spirits inhabited the waters. The prophet Ezekiel by the spirit of Prophecy revealed this.

"Speak, and say, Thus saith the Lord GOD; Behold, I [am] against thee, Pharaoh king of Egypt, the great dragon that lieth in the midst of his rivers, which hath said, My river [is] mine own, and I have made [it] for myself" (Ezekiel 29:3 KJV)

PERSON-PORTALS

Not only are spiritual portals locations, but a person can be a portal into the realm of the spirit. These people carry what is known as open heavens over their lives and wherever they appear an open heaven is created. When you get in contact with such personalities miracles and the manifestation of the supernatural are evident.

In the Bible there were certain men who were portals:

Jesus was a Person-Portal when He walked the earth. He brought heaven on earth. He was a medium and a channel to the realm of the spirit. When people got into His presence they were healed. Miracles and supernatural events happened in His presence. Demons cried and trembled in his presence.

"And there was in their synagogue a man with an unclean spirit; and he cried out, Saying, Let [us] alone; what have we to do with thee, thou Jesus of Nazareth? art thou come to destroy us? I know thee who thou art, the Holy One of God. And Jesus rebuked him, saying, Hold thy peace, and come out of him" (Mark 1:23-25 KJV).

Jesus was a Person-portal when He was around the shores of Galilee. There was an open heaven over His life. Angels were trafficking over Him.

"And he saith unto him, Verily, verily, I say unto you, Hereafter ye shall see heaven open, and the angels of God ascending and descending upon the

Son of man" (John 1:51 KJV).

Now because Jesus is a Person-Portal, by Him we have access to God the Father and the throne room. He has opened the heavens for all of mankind.

"For through him we both <u>have access</u> by one Spirit unto the Father" (Ephesians 2:18 KJV)

"Therefore being justified by faith, we have peace with God through our Lord Jesus Christ: By whom also <u>we have access by faith</u> into this grace wherein we stand, and rejoice in hope of the glory of God" (Romans 5:1-2 KJV)

By Jesus we have access to the heavenly realms. Jesus Himself said He was the way to the Father. *"Jesus saith unto him, <u>I am the way</u>, the truth, and the life: no man cometh unto the Father, but by me" (John 14:6 KJV)*

This means He is the opening, doorway and entrance to the heavenly dimension. He forms the connection or communicating channel to the spiritual realm.

Certain men of God served as Person-portals. One common example is Charles Grandison Finney who lived in the 19th Century. He was an American minister and the leader in the second great awakening. It is said of him that when he arrived in a city the whole city would be gripped with the presence of God. When he was in a city the whole city was involved as shopkeepers closed down their businesses and urged people to attend his meetings. An entire region would be affected when Finney was around. Some of the hardcore sinners would be saved. Alcoholic bars and club houses shut down.

This is because he was a Person-Portal. He carried a heavenly atmosphere. He had open heavens over his life. As one man he was an invasion of heaven on earth.

OBJECT -PORTALS

Objects too can serve as portals. Such objects are portals or points of contact to the supernatural. In the book of Acts handkerchiefs and aprons became object portals when they made contact with the Apostle Paul.

"And God wrought special miracles by the hands of Paul: So that from his body were brought unto the sick handkerchiefs or aprons, and the diseases departed from them, and the evil spirits went out of them" (Acts 19:11-12 KJV).

There are several objects which can serve as demonic portals. Old paintings and artifacts can serve as portals into the realm of the spirit. I heard the story of a man who travelled to Haiti, a country in the Caribbean. He saw a very nice stick in the market and he bought it. The moment he brought the stick to his house he got a severe spinal disease. In prayer God told him the source of the disease was the stick he got from Haiti. The moment he got rid of the stick the disease vanished.

What was happening? The stick was an object portal to the demonic.

Also, certain jewels handed down from one generation to another can be object portals. It can be necklaces, beads, chairs or pictures. You must be very spiritual and sensitive to the spirit of God. I believe if a person is sensitive to the Holy Spirit, He will show him/her what objects must be dealt with.

Certain books are demonic portals especially books that teach and talk about witchcraft. Parents must be careful and sensitive to the kind of books their children read. An example of such books is the Harry Potter series.

Certain horror movies can also serve as demonic portals. Ouija boards are an example of objects which serve as demonic portal.

In the same way, the Bible is also a portal to the realm of the spirit. The bible is a very great portal. Just by reading the Bible you can have revelations and spiritual experiences and encounters.

Your pillow and your bed can serve as a portal into the supernatural realm if you take time and consecrate them to God. Jacob picked up a stone for a pillow, and the stone became a portal into the spiritual realm.

"And he lighted upon a certain place, and tarried there all night, because the sun was set; and he took of the stones of that place, and put [them for] his pillows, and lay down in that place to sleep. And he dreamed, and behold a ladder set up on the earth, and the top of it reached to heaven: and behold the angels of God ascending and descending on it" (Genesis 28:11-12 KJV)

TIME-ZONE PORTALS

Certain time zones or periods serve as portals into the realm of the spirit. Such time periods and zones are what is called "the Junctions of time." And that is the subject of this book. The subsequent chapters will throw more light on it.

HOW TO CREATE PORTALS

Portals can be created, and the focus is on godly portals.

Increased spiritual activities at location can create a spiritual portal. Your house can become a location-portal if you pray intense prayers there. Some people have certain rooms in their homes designated as Prayer rooms. Such rooms easily serve as Location-Portals if great amounts of time is spent there in intense prayer.

Every born-again child of God can be a Person-Portal like Jesus for the scriptures declare, as He is so are we in this world.

"...because as he is, so are we in this world" (1 John 4:17 KJV)

If as believer in the Lord Jesus Christ we spent quality time in the presence of God in prayers and fasting like Jesus, open heavens will be created strongly. I actually believe every believer is Person-portal, but the intensity of the manifestation differs from one believer to another. And the difference is based on the price we are willing to pay.

Practicing daily prayer, frequent fasting and sacrificial giving will create great spiritual portals for any believer.

Such believers become living, walking and talking altars of God. Hallelujah!

CHAPTER 3

DEFINITION OF TERMS

JUNCTIONS OF TIME

A junction is a point where two or more things meet or converge. It's a region of transition. It is an intersection. So, what then are the junctions of time?

Junctions of time are times of the day or night with heightened specific spiritual activities. There are certain times of the day which serve as entry points into the realm of the spirit and those times are called the junctions of time. They are portals into the spiritual realm.

The same way we have junctions on highways, even so there are junctions on the traffic of time. We have a 24-hour time period with junctions and those are what are called the junctions of time where specific spiritual events happen and take place easily.

For example, Jesus on His day of crucifixion was arrested at night. He was mocked and beaten from dawn. He carried the cruel roman cross to Golgotha on an empty stomach. And finally, he had both hands and feet nailed to the cross. Actually, the way Jesus was treated He should have died earlier in the day. But He would not give up the ghost till a specific time zone. When that time finally came, He gave up the Ghost. He wouldn't die before that time which was 3PM. Jesus knew the junctions of time and took advantage of them.

Once you know what happens in the junctions of time, you can also take advantage of it and maximize the results you get in the realm of the spirit.

In the USA for example, federal taxes are supposed to be filed by the 15th of April every year. So, the Internal Revenue Service (IRS) gets very busy from January to April. That is not to say they don't work throughout the year. They work all year round but their activities are heightened in that time period.

On the highway of time, there is a lot that happens within a 24-hour period but there are specific portions (junctions) where specific spiritual beings are very active and specific events happen.

Demonic agents, witches and wizards work throughout the day. But everyone is aware that their activities are heightened in the night season. Because they are agents of darkness they wait for that junction of time because it enhances their work and activities. Those who practice astral projection wait for certain seasons of the day or night to do their work. There are certain seasons when the realm of the spirit is congested with people practicing astral projections. It's like on the highways, there are seasons called rush hours when there is heavy traffic and other times where the traffic has eased.

Now when we talk about the junctions of time we are not saying that God will not hear you when you pray at different times of the day or the night. But when we talk about the junctions of time, you are going to take advantage of the heightened specific spiritual activities at that particular time. You can pray anytime during the day or the night and God will hear and answer. But your knowledge of the junctions of time will enhance your prayer life.

Once I needed a drastic victory concerning a matter. I prayed about it for several days. Then suddenly the Holy Spirit told me to pray and praise at night from 12 midnight to 3AM. I did exactly that and by morning I had already obtained the victory.

Taking advantage of the junctions of time empowers and enhances prayer.

WATCHERS

In the book of Daniel, Nebuchadnezzar the Babylonian King had a night vision. The vision was given or brought to him by a Watcher. The Bible declares that the watcher was a holy one which came down from Heaven.

"I saw in the visions of my head upon my bed, and, behold, <u>a watcher and an holy one</u> came down from heaven" (Daniel 4:13 KJV).

In verse seventeen of the same chapter, we realize that the Watcher that appeared to King Nebuchadnezzar came to talk to him about time. The Watcher said, let seven times pass over him. The Watcher made the decree and gave the verdict concerning the times of King Nebuchadnezzar.

"Let his heart be changed from man's, and let a beast's heart be given unto him; <u>and let seven times pass over him</u>. This matter [is] by the decree of the watchers, and the demand by the word of the holy

ones: to the intent that the living may know that the most High ruleth in the kingdom of men, and giveth it to whomsoever he will, and setteth up over it the basest of men." (Daniel 4:16-17 KJV)

Who are the Watchers? The Watchers are a class of Angels in charge of Time. They are the Wakeful ones. Don't forget that angels come in classes, companies, and groups.

"But ye are come unto mount Sion, and unto the city of the living God, the heavenly Jerusalem, and to an innumerable <u>company</u> of angels" (Hebrews 12:22 KJV)

The angels come in groups. In the above verse the adjective innumerable is qualifying the company, not the angels. This means the groups of angels cannot be counted. And each group or set of angels is innumerable. To actually count the number of angels would be innumerable times innumerable.

There is a company or class of angels in charge of healing. Another company in charge of warfare. Another in charge of finances. You don't have one angel doing everything. There is very fine specialization in the angelic order. For example, in the hospital, we have doctors who have specialize in the study or treatment of heart disease and abnormalities. He/she is a cardiologist. Another specializes in the functions and disorders of the nervous system. And such a doctor is called a neurologist. The cardiologist is a doctor. The neurologist is also a doctor. But they handle or fix specific disorders in the human body. In the same way angels have different specialties.

One angel cannot and does not do everything.

Now the Watchers are a class of angels that are in charge of time. They determine the seasons and times of individuals, nations, governments, institutions and families. This class of angels are in charge of the dispensations of God. They have the power to change governments of nations.

If you know how to work with them, you can change seasons in your life.

A WATCHMAN

In the bible days all the cities had huge walls around them.

"And it shall come to pass, that when they make a long [blast] with the ram's horn, [and] when ye hear the sound of the trumpet, all the people shall shout with a great shout; and the wall of the city shall fall down flat, and the people shall ascend up every man straight before him" (Joshua 6:5 KJV)

The city of Jericho had a huge wall. Those walls were very thick walls and it had houses in them. To have a house in a wall meant the wall was pretty huge. It is believed that six chariots of horses could run horizontally on it.

"Then she let them down by a cord through the window: for her house [was] upon the town wall, and she dwelt upon the wall" (Joshua 2:15 KJV)

Now the walls had gates in them. The gates were opened during the day to allow people to get in and out of the cities for business and other errands. At night time, the gates were closed. The walls in those days were very significant. When you had a great wall, it signified that the city was very fortified. Strong and fortified walls were also a sign of economic prosperity. This was so, because a lot of money was needed to build a great wall. Due to these reasons, when Nehemiah heard about deterioration in the walls of Jerusalem he was saddened and cried.

Now in the walls there were what was known as Watch towers. There were men, most of the time soldiers, who ran shifts day and night to watch over the city. These men stayed in the Watch tower. And they observed if there was any danger coming to the city. When they noticed anything of the sort they would report to the city and the report would eventually get to the King. The whole city would prepare for the danger.

The men who stayed in the Watch tower were known as the Watchmen. One is known as a Watchman. These men were set by the walls on specific times of the day and night. They were like city guards or city patrols. They were the sentinels of their day. These men were the eyes and the ears of the city and they were set over the city, especially at night.

Let's consider certain scriptures that talk about a watchman or watchmen.

1. The watchman looked or observed
"And <u>the watchmen</u> of Saul in Gibeah of Benjamin looked; and, behold, the multitude melted away, and

they went on beating down [one another]" (1 Samuel 14:16 KJV)

2. The Watchman stood and occupied the watch tower
"And there stood a <u>watchman on the tower</u> in Jezreel, and he spied the company of Jehu as he came, and said, I see a company. And Joram said, Take an horseman, and send to meet them, and let him say, [Is it] peace?" (2 Kings 9:17 KJV).

3. The watchmen keep watch
"But Absalom fled. And the <u>young man that kept the watch</u> lifted up his eyes, and looked, and, behold, there came much people by the way of the hill side behind him" (2 Samuel 13:34 KJV)

4. The Watchmen stand upon the walls. They are not supposed to rest day nor night.
"I have set <u>watchmen upon thy walls</u>, O Jerusalem, [which] shall never hold their peace day nor night: ye that make mention of the LORD, keep not silence" (Isaiah 62:6 KJV)

The watchman must always be vigilant. They carried news either good or bad into the city. Their role was very important and it could not be underestimated.

HOW DO YOU BECOME A SPIRITUAL WATCHMAN

Someone may be asking how do I become a watchman because my city does not have walls? You can become a Spiritual Watchman by KEEPING WATCH. The watchmen in bible days kept watch.

And you cannot keep watch without understanding the junctions of time. The Junctions of time are the watch towers you stand on to watch. And the moment you begin to observe the watches, angelic watchers begin to work with you. Anytime you pray at the junctions of time, be rest assured that the watchers are present to operate with you.

Just as men stood and patrolled the city walls in the bible days to watch for signs, danger and what the enemy was doing, this present-day, spiritual watchmen must climb on the spiritual watch tower and also watch. And in the same way the watchmen did not look at just the bad things coming but also good things, we must also watch for what God is doing in our lives, and know the agenda of God in our time. You can become a spiritual watchman for your nation, city, or family. You can see and discern the agenda of heaven for your people by watching.

To be a spiritual watchman you must WATCH.

WHAT DOES IT MEANS TO WATCH?

To watch simply means to pray. Almost anytime you see Watch in the bible it goes with prayer, especially in the New Testament.

1. *"Watch and pray, that ye enter not into temptation: the spirit indeed [is] willing, but the flesh [is] weak" (Matthew 26:41 KJV).*

2. *"Take ye heed, watch and pray: for ye know not when the time is" (Mark 13:33 KJV)*

3. *"Continue in <u>prayer,</u> and <u>watch</u> in the same with thanksgiving" (Colossians 4:2 KJV)*

4. *"But the end of all things is at hand: be ye therefore sober, and <u>watch unto prayer</u>" (1 Peter 4:7 KJV)*

Anytime you see *Prayer* you see *Watch* and anytime you see *Watch* you see *Prayer*. Spiritual watchmen are men and women who watch, meaning they stand upon the junctions of time and pray.

The Prophet Habakkuk made a statement about standing upon his watch in the second chapter of his book.

"I will stand upon my watch, and set me upon the tower, and will watch to see what he will say unto me, and what I shall answer when I am reproved" (Habakkuk 2:1 KJV)

Based on the understanding gained so far, what he meant by standing upon his watch simply means he would stand and pray. And by saying, *I will watch to see,* he meant *I will pray to see.* The means of seeing visions is to enter into prayer. And when you enter into prayer at the junctions of time you are sure to see visions.

Habakkuk said I will stand upon my watch and that was how Prophet Habakkuk had visions from the Lord. He shared his secret with us right there.

CHAPTER 4

THE DIVISIONS OF THE DAY AND THE NIGHT

You may be asking so what prayers do I pray at the junctions of time? How do I benefit from the Junctions of time? We are moving closer to greater understanding & how you can take advantage of the junctions of time.

DISCLAIMER

But first I have a disclaimer to make. I am not teaching in this book that there are only certain times of the day that you can pray specific prayers. I am not saying that God will only listen to your prayers at particular points in time. God will listen to you at any time.

The junctions of time are periods of *heightened* specific spiritual activities. They are points of high specific spiritual energy. Praying at these times is an added advantage to your prayer life. The heightened spiritual activity enables and enhances prayer. This is because in prayer you are engaging the spiritual energy of God.

Now the Junctions of time is what is popularly called Watches. You may have heard of it before. The expression normally used is *Observing the Watches*. The time has been divided into windows or specific time zones where you pray specific kinds of prayers at particular times. Traditionally, it is said that there are eight watches. But that is where this book deviates from the traditional view and sticks to the Bible. The bible does not reveal eight watches. Stay with me as we examine what the scriptures teach.

DAY AND NIGHT

24- hours makes a complete day cycle. This 24 hours is divided into two segments. We have the Day time that is governed or ruled by Light, and the Night time which is ruled by darkness.

The Day is from 6.00 AM TO 6.00 PM. The Night is from 6.00 PM to 6.00 AM. Actually, it was God who divided the day from the night.

"And God said, Let there be light: and there was light. And God saw the light, that [it was] good: and God divided the light from the darkness. And God called the light Day, and the darkness he called Night. And the evening and the morning were the first day" *(Genesis 1:3-5 KJV).*

THE SUN AND MOON WERE MADE TO RULE

God was the one who made the lights—the sun and the moon. God made them for a reason. God does everything for a purpose. There is nothing God ever made without a purpose.

The first reason for the Lights God made was to divide the Day from the Night.

"And God said, Let there be lights in the firmament of the heaven to divide the day from the night; and let them be for signs, and for seasons, and for days, and years:" (Genesis 1:14 KJV).

The second important reason for the Lights God made is for ruling.

"And God made two great lights; the greater light to rule the day, and the lesser light to rule the night: [he made] the stars also" (Genesis 1:16 KJV)

God made the greater light which is the Sun to rule the day and the Lesser light which is the Moon to rule the night. God gave an order to the Sun and the Moon to rule. That is the mandate God them; to rule the day and night. According to the scriptures the sun rules and the moon rules. The sun is not in the skies just to shine. The Moon is not there just to shine at night. We must have an understanding of the elements God created and their purposes. Don't forget God gave man dominion over all His creation and that includes the sun and the moon. But God also gave the sun and the moon a ruling ability.

JESUS MUST RULE YOUR DAY AND NIGHT

As said earlier, the sun must rule the day and the moon and the stars must rule the night.

"The sun to rule by day: for his mercy [endureth] for ever: The moon and stars to rule by night: for his mercy [endureth] for ever" (Psalms 136:8-9 KJV)

A ruler dictates the happenings and direct affairs of a people or a place. God in His great plan and wisdom wants to rule your day and night.

"The sun shall be no more thy light by day; neither for brightness shall the moon give light unto thee: but the LORD shall be unto thee an everlasting light, and thy God thy glory" (Isaiah 60:19 KJV)

As a result, Jesus Christ has become your Sun if you are a believer. He now rules your day and directs your steps. He is the Lord. Prophet Malachi said, He has become the Sun of Righteousness

"But unto you that fear my name shall the Sun of righteousness arise with healing in his wings; and ye shall go forth, and grow up as calves of the stall" (Malachi 4:2 KJV)

Not only is Jesus your Sun to rule your day, He is also the Star to rule your night.

"I Jesus have sent mine angel to testify unto you these things in the churches. I am the root and the offspring of David, [and] the bright and morning star" (Revelation 22:16 KJV)

You must make declarations that Jesus is your sun that rules your day and the Bright Star that rules your night. Declare that the physical sun will not smite you by day nor the moon by night. But instead the SUN of Righteousness and the Bright and Morning Star blesses and preserves you by day and by night respectively.

CHAPTER 5

WATCHES ARE OF THE NIGHT NOT OF THE DAY

The night is divided into four watches according to the scriptures. Traditionally, most people also divide the day into watches but when we examine scriptures, you don't find that the day is divided into watches. It is basically the night which is divided into watches. Almost anytime the expression 'a watch' is used in the bible it is used in reference to the night. You always find a watch of the night. Hardly do you come across a watch of the day. Let's examine this with several scriptures.

1. *"For a thousand years in thy sight [are but] as yesterday when it is past, and [as] <u>a watch in the night</u>" (Psalms 90:4 KJV)*

Notice: a watch in the night not a watch in the day.

2. *"On my bed I remember you; I think of you through the <u>watches of the night</u>" (Psalms 63:6 NIV).*
"My eyes stay open through the <u>watches of the night</u>, that I may meditate on your promises" (Psalms 119:148 NIV).

The Psalms say he meditates in the watches of the night, not of the day. Again, *watch* is used in reference to the night and not the day.

3. *"And there were in the same country shepherds abiding in the field, keeping watch over their flock by*

night" (Luke 2:8 KJV)

The shepherds kept or observed the watch but it was by night, not during the day.

4. *"But know this, that if the goodman of the house had known in what watch the thief would come, he would have watched, and would not have suffered his house to be broken up" (Matthew 24:43 KJV)*

"For yourselves know perfectly that the day of the Lord so cometh as a thief in the night" (1 Thessalonians 5:2 KJV)

From the two verses above we know that the thief comes in the night. And the goodman of house if he had known what watch the thief would come would not have slept. Here again we see watch used in reference to the night and not the day.

So typically watches are in reference to the night and not the day.

THE FOUR WATCHES OF THE NIGHT

Now let's identify the four-night watches. Actually, Jesus was the one who revealed them to us in the New Testament. You might be thinking it is only in the Old Testament where Watchmen and the Watches and mentioned. Not at all. Further examination of the New Testament helps us discover that the apostles of the Lord Jesus used to pray at the junctions of time.

"Watch ye therefore: for ye know not when the master of the house cometh, at even, or at midnight, or at the cockcrowing, or in the morning" (Mark 13:35 KJV)

Here are the four watches:

1.First Watch of the Night is also called the Evening Watch.
2. Second Watch of the Night is also called the Midnight Watch.
3.Third Watch of the Night is also called the Cockcrowing Watch
4.Fourth Watch of the Night is also called the Morning or Dawn Watch.

This is the classification given by Jesus.

As we stated earlier, the night is from 6.00PM TO 6.00AM. There are twelve hours in the night and it is divided into four watches.

1. First Watch/Evening Watch -6.00PM to 9.00PM
2. Second Watch/Midnight Watch- 9.00PM to 12 MIDNIGHT
3. Third Watch/Cockcrowing Watch -12 MIDNIGHT to 3.00AM
4. Fourth Watch/Morning Watch/Dawn Watch- 3.00AM to 6.00AM

Now if you study the gospels you will realize that Jesus made several references to the watches in His teachings.

"And if he shall come in the second watch, or come in the third watch, and find [them] so, blessed are those servants" (Luke 12:38 KJV)

In the above verse Jesus makes mention of the second and third watches. Now you know exactly the time periods to which he was referring.

Now there are specific spiritual activities that happen at each of these watches. The reason those specific things happen is because particular portals are opened in time at those defined seasons or junctions which heightens the specific spiritual energies. For example, most people know that witches and wizards fly and work a lot at night. If you don't know I'm sure you have seen it depicted in a movie. Why do they have to wait until Midnight to work? Why don't they fly at 3PM? This doesn't mean they don't work at other times. But there are peak witchcraft activities at midnight. Why? Because they are agents of darkness and they function effectively in the dark. The spiritual energy at that time is optimal for their operations. They take advantage of the atmosphere at that time because the darkness at that hour serves as a portal into the realm of the spirit.

In the same way as a believer in the Lord Jesus, you can pray anytime and all the time. But knowing what happens at specific junctions of time allows you to pray specific prayers at specified times. And when you practice matching your prayers to the specific Watches you will see a great deal of results.

Consider this, in the land of Egypt when God was bringing deliverance to the Israelites, He told Moses that the angel of death was coming to kill the firstborn sons of the Egyptians. Now the angel of death did not come in the morning or afternoon. It didn't even come at 9PM. It waited till midnight. God would not allow the angel of death to come until midnight. I believe that God, being the creator of time and knowing the junctions in time and the specific energies at each junction, specifically chose midnight.

We have discovered the four watches already in this chapters. In the subsequent chapters of this book we will learn the specific activities that happen at each watch and the specific prayers to pray at these times.

Now let's explore the general prayers and activities for all the night watches.

GENERAL PRAYERS AND ACTIVITIES FOR ALL THE NIGHT WATCHES

Now there are certain prayers and spiritual activities you can do in any of the four watches. You can do them and pray them either in the first, second, third or the fourth watch.

1. *Receive Instructions from your heart in the Night watches.*

"I will praise the LORD, who counsels me; <u>even at night</u> my heart instructs me" (Psalms 16:7 NIV)

One very important thing you have to be conscious of is that in the night season you get a lot of instructions from God. That is not to say that God cannot speak to you during the day. But in the night season a lot of instructions are released. It is very easy to access instructions at night. In the scripture above why didn't David say *in the day season?* This is because in the night watches the spiritual energy is conducive for receiving instructions easily. Maybe you are looking for an instruction about your destiny or trying to access a divine idea. Give a lot of attention in the night season. Take advantage of the night and set yourself apart knowing that in the night season your heart will certainly instruct you. It can happen either in the first, second, third or fourth watch.

2. Receive Visions in the Night.

"For God speaketh once, yea twice, [yet man] perceiveth it not. In a dream, in a vision of the night, when deep sleep falleth upon men, in slumberings upon the bed" (Job 33:14-15 KJV)

Expect dreams and visions from God at night. Though you can sleep in the daytime, dreams and visions abound in the night watches.

Jacob had a dramatic vision from God on his way to his uncle Laban's house. In that vision of the night he received prophetic words concerning his destiny.

"And he lighted upon a certain place, and tarried there __all night__, because the sun was set; and he took of the stones of that place, and put [them for] his pillows, and lay down in that place to sleep. __And he dreamed__, and behold a ladder set up on the earth, and the top of it reached to heaven: and behold the angels of God ascending and descending on it. And, behold, the

LORD stood above it, and said, I [am] the LORD God of Abraham thy father, and the God of Isaac: the land whereon thou liest, to thee will I give it, and to thy seed" (Genesis 28:11-13 KJV)

God appeared to Solomon in a vision of the night and asked Solomon to ask for anything. This happened after Solomon sacrificed a thousand burnt offerings to the Lord.

"In Gibeon the LORD appeared to Solomon in a dream by night: and God said, Ask what I shall give thee" (1 Kings 3:5 KJV)

Knowing this, you can take advantage of the night season to receive visions and encounters from God. Visions abound in the night because specific spiritual activities are heightened.

3. Pray against Terrors and Pestilence In the night watches.

"Thou shalt not be afraid for the terror by night; [nor] for the arrow [that] flieth by day; [Nor] for the pestilence [that] walketh in darkness; [nor] for the destruction [that] wasteth at noonday" (Psalms 91:5-6 KJV)

In the night watches pray and come against terrors and pestilence. This is because they are released at night and in darkness. Arrows and destruction are of the day but terrors and pestilence are of the night. So, take time off and handle them at night. Terrors and pestilence are a demonic class which operate at night. There is class of demonic spirits called terrors. And another one called pestilence.

When a Terror spirit strikes you or attacks you, they inject fear in you. The best time to wage war in prayer against such spirits is in the night seasons. Pray in the name of Jesus against every spirit of terror or pestilence that is released against your life, family, education, business, finances or ministry.

It is also a good time to pray against terrorist attacks and activities throughout the world. Understand and know that most of the terrorist activities are demonic and the spirits involved are the terrors.

4. Meditate in the night watches.

"When I remember thee upon my bed, [and] meditate on thee in the [night] watches" (Psalms 63:6 KJV)

"Mine eyes prevent the [night] watches, that I might meditate in thy word" (Psalms 119:148 KJV)

The night watches are good for meditation. David practiced meditation especially at night. David was a wonder to his world and a man after the heart of God and I believe this was one of his secrets. Don't spend all your night seasons watching the television and sleeping. Most of the time God comes to wake you up to meditate but because you are not sensitive, you just continue to sleep.

5. Sing and Remember God's Faithfulness in the Night Watches.

"To shew forth thy lovingkindness in the morning,

and thy faithfulness every night" (Psalms 92:2 KJV)

"To announce your love each daybreak, sing your faithful presence all through the night" (Psalms 92:2 MSG)

In the night watches don't forget about God's faithfulness. Sing songs that tell of His faithfulness. Walk through the bible and see the amazing faithfulness of God displayed to His servants of old. Look and consider your own life and discover how faithful God has been to you and your family.

6. Pray and stop the works of the thief in the Night Watches.

"For yourselves know perfectly that the day of the Lord so cometh as a thief in the night"
(1 Thessalonians 5:2 KJV)

The thief comes in the night season. So, in the night watches pray and stop his works. What are the works of the thief? Jesus told us of them:

"The thief cometh not, but for to steal, and to kill, and to destroy..." (John 10:10 KJV)

The thief comes to steal, kill and destroy. Pray and prevent the thief from stealing your joy, miracle, marriage and destiny. Stop strategies of the thief to kill your job and anyone or anything in your life. Stop the work of the destroyer.

The spiritual energies and portals opened at night cause

the thief to step out. You must stop his works. Doing a lot of spiritual warfare at night yields great results.

7. Stand in the house of the Lord and Bless Him in the night watches.

"Behold, bless ye the LORD, all [ye] servants of the LORD, which by night stand in the house of the LORD" (Psalms 134:1 KJV)

You stand in the house of the Lord in the night watches. Someone might be asking; does it mean I have to go to the church building and stand there? Not really. But if your church has evening services, it would be good to attend.

What you need to do is to meditate on the house of the Lord which will stir up praises from your heart. Now you should not be thinking of a physical building as the house of the Lord. *You* are the temple of the Lord. You have become the dwelling and abode of the Lord. Think and become aware that God lives in you now.

"Know ye not that ye are the temple of God, and [that] the Spirit of God dwelleth in you? (1 Corinthians 3:16 KJV).

The night season is a good time to pray for your local church. Pray for its leaders, its growth and impact. It is also the time to pray for the body of Christ all over the world.

Now in the next chapter we will examine the four watches of the night and explore them in more depth. We will discover the prayers to pray and the spiritual activities to engage.

CHAPTER 6

SPECIFIC PRAYERS TO PRAY AT EACH WATCH OF THE NIGHT

We have discovered from the previous chapter that there are four watches. These are:

1. First Watch/Evening Watch -6.00 PM to 9.00 PM
2. Second Watch/Midnight Watch- 9.00 PM to 12 MIDNIGHT
3. Third Watch/Cockcrowing Watch -12 MIDNIGHT to 3.00 AM
4. Fourth Watch/Morning Watch/Dawn Watch- 3.00 AM to 6.00 AM

We have also learned the general prayer points which can be prayed for all the night seasons. In this chapter we will begin to study the prayers for the specific watches of the night.

Now in observing the watches or praying at the Junctions of time, you don't necessarily have to pray throughout the entire window of time. For example, in the first watch you can pray anywhere between 6.00 PM to 9.00 PM, for any amount of time within that window. Or you can pray the whole three hours if you can.

FIRST WATCH/EVENING WATCH - 6.00 PM to 9.00 PM

1. YOU POUR OUT YOUR HEART TO THE LORD

You pray at the beginning of the watches. You cry out to God. And to cry out is to pray. This is a time to have a heart to heart talk with God. *"Arise, cry out in the night: in the beginning of the watches pour out thine heart like water before the face of the Lord" (Lamentations 2:19a KJV)*

2. *YOU PRAY FOR CHILDREN AND THE YOUTH*

In this watch you pray for your children and all the children you know. It is also a good time to pray for the youth across your city and the world at large. You pray for the youth to be fed with the word of God. You pray for a hunger and a thirst for young people. Desire for the Holy spirit to have a strong move among the youth and children. Pray for the preservation of your sons and daughters and tell God to use them as vessels unto honor.

"Arise, cry out in the night: in the beginning of the watches pour out thine heart like water before the face of the Lord: lift up thy hands toward him for the life of thy young children, that faint for hunger in the top of every street" (Lamentations 2:19 KJV)

3. *YOU PRAY FOR ORPHANS, HOMELESS AND STREET CHILDREN*

This is also the time to pray for all orphans, homeless children and street children in your city, country and world. There are a lot of children all over the world who live on the streets. Such children are very vulnerable. And you must pray for them in this watch. *"Arise, cry out in the night: in the beginning of the watches pour out thine*

heart like water before the face of the Lord: <u>lift up thy</u>
<u>hands toward him for the life of thy young children,</u>
<u>that faint for hunger in the top of every street</u>"
(Lamentations 2:19 KJV)

4. *PRAY FOR THE HEALING OF SICK*
PEOPLE AROUND THE WORLD

This a good time to pray and intercede for sick people.
Jesus healed a lot of sick folks in the evening. Most of His
mass healings happen in the evening. That is not to say He
never healed the sick at other times. But a lot of healing
took place in the evening. I believe that is why most healing
evangelists have healing crusades in the evenings. At
evening the healing dinner is set because healing is the food
for the children.

"And at even, when the sun did set, they brought
unto him all that were diseased, and them that were
possessed with devils" (Mark 1:32 KJV).

"Now when the sun was setting, all they that had
any sick with divers diseases brought them unto him;
and he laid his hands on every one of them, and
healed them" (Luke 4:40 KJV)

5. *PRAY AND HANDLE DEMONIC ROBBERS*
AND SPOILERS

This is the hour to pray and handle the enemy and the
adversaries that spoil and rob you of your destiny. They are
called destiny robbers. Those who oppose you in your
divine assignment must be dealt with now. As you pray,
God will release trouble to such beings. *"And behold at*

eveningtide trouble; [and] before the morning he [is] not. This [is] the portion of them that spoil us, and the lot of them that rob us" (Isaiah 17:14 KJV)

6. PRAY AND SILENCE DEMONIC DOGS AND WITCHCRAFT ACTIVITY

Silence the noise of demonic dogs released in your city. The noise of these spirits is to release curses unto families, children, businesses and cities. You need to silence them in this watch. You pray and stop them with the fire of God in their tracks because such demonic dogs roam about in the city. Pray to put chains and padlocks upon their mouths to silence them so that they can't make their noise. Silence them so that they can't speak against your destiny, children, business and family.

"They return at evening: they make a noise like a dog, and go round about the city" (Psalms 59:6 KJV).

7. TAKE CHARGE OF THE GATEWAY TO THE NIGHT

The first watch or the evening watch is the foundation of the Night season. It is the gateway to the night. All the activities in the night seasons start at this time. Anytime your watch hits 6:00 pm, you want to say, "In the name of Jesus, I take charge of the night season. No demonic activity can prevail against my children, my family, my church, my destiny or my assignment in Jesus' name." Just by that statement you have taken possession of the gates of the night. You want to make sure the foundations are kept.

"If the foundations be destroyed, what can the righteous do? (Psalms 11:3 KJV)

SECOND WATCH/MIDNIGHT WATCH 9.00 PM TO 12 MIDNIGHT

1. PRAY TO RECEIVE GRACE TO FULFILL YOUR GOD-GIVEN ASSIGNMENT

This is the season to pray concerning your assignment and purpose in life. There are times you lose zeal and fervor in your assignment, but when you pray God will give you more grace. With more grace you will be alert and the Lord will find you fulfilling your mandate when He returns. Pray to receive strength to run your race and finish your course.

"Blessed [are] those servants, whom the lord when he cometh shall find watching: verily I say unto you, that he shall gird himself, and make them to sit down to meat, and will come forth and serve them. And if he shall come in the second watch, or come in the third watch, and find [them] so, blessed are those servants" *(Luke 12:37-38 KJV)*

2. PRAY FOR DIVINE PROTECTION

This is also the season for praying for Divine protection for your yourself and your family. You pray for protection in all your travels and dealings. Divine protection was released for Paul, the apostle at this hour because there were plans to take his life. pray for preservation of life and possession.

"Then he called two of his centurions and ordered them, "Get ready a detachment of two hundred soldiers, seventy horsemen and two hundred spearmen to go to Caesarea <u>at nine tonight</u>"
(Acts 23:23 NIV)

3. PRAY FOR DIVINE PROVISION

You can also pray for divine provision for your life's journey. The centurion made great provisions for Paul at this hour. A beast was provided for Paul the apostle for transportation. I believe if it was in our day it would have been a Mercedes Benz or Toyota Land Cruiser.

"And provide for them beasts, that they may set Paul on, and bring him safe to Felix the governor"
(Acts 23:24 KJV)

THIRD WATCH/COCKCROWING WATCH
12 MIDNIGHT TO 3.00 AM

1. GIVE THANKS AND SING PRAISES IN THIS WATCH.

King David practiced getting up at 12 midnight to give thanks to God. I believe it is one of the things that made David a success. Thank God for everything He is to you and done for you. *"At <u>midnight</u> I will rise to give thanks unto thee because of thy righteous judgments"* *(Psalms 119:62 KJV)*.

Paul and Silas also sang praises to God at this watch. This is a good time to sing praises and dance before God

THE JUNCTIONS OF TIME

especially when you need victory concerning an issue. Paul
and Silas needed a dramatic turnaround of things and they
sang praise at this Watch. You might not be able to do this
every night, but when there is an issue confronting you and
you must get your victory then you must engage the portals
of time.

In the year 2012, I needed a great miracle desperately. I
had fasted and prayed and yet I had no peace about the
matter. Then the Spirit of God directed me to sing praises
in this Watch. So, at midnight I picked up the documents
involved in the matter in my living room. And I sang praise
and danced for three hours all by myself. The moment I
was through, I got the note of victory in my heart. And
eventually I got the victory in time.

Midnight thanksgiving and praise releases great power.
Practice it.

*"And at midnight Paul and Silas prayed, and sang
praises unto God: and the prisoners heard them" (Acts
16:25 KJV)*

2. COMMAND A DIVINE RELEASE OF THE CAPTIVES

Pray for the release of anyone the enemy has held
captive. It can be any form of captivity or bondage. Those
in bondage of drugs, sin and hell demand their release in
the name of Jesus. Pray and release anything of yours the
devil has held captive.

If you have relatives who have been imprisoned, demand
a miraculous release in this hour.

"And at midnight Paul and Silas prayed, and sang praises unto God: and the prisoners heard them" *(Acts 16:25 KJV)*

"And brought them out, and said, Sirs, what must I do to be saved? (Acts 16:30 KJV)

3. PRAY AND BREAK CHRONIC BONDAGES AND JUDGEMENT OVER THE ENEMY

The Israelites got their deliverance at midnight. It was at midnight that God brought the final judgment on Egypt who were the arch enemies of the Israelites. Pray and release the final judgment of God in the camp of the enemy. And then demand the final deliverance of your children, husband, wife and family. The age-long bondage of Egypt over Israel was broken at midnight. Midnight is an amazing time to pray.

"And it came to pass, that at midnight the LORD smote all the firstborn in the land of Egypt, from the firstborn of Pharaoh that sat on his throne unto the firstborn of the captive that [was] in the dungeon; and all the firstborn of cattle. And Pharaoh rose up in the night, he, and all his servants, and all the Egyptians; and there was a great cry in Egypt; for [there was] not a house where [there was] not one dead. And he called for Moses and Aaron by night, and said, Rise up, [and] get you forth from among my people, both ye and the children of Israel; and go, serve the LORD, as ye have said" (Exodus 12:29-31 KJV)

4. PRAY FOR DIVINE FAVOR

Pray for uncommon favor over your life and destiny. The Israelites had great favor during this Watch after their release. If you have an interview of any sort this is a good time to pray. Release the angels in charge of favor to work for you. If you can organize favor for yourself at midnight in the morning everyone and everything must favor you.

"And the children of Israel did according to the word of Moses; and they borrowed of the Egyptians jewels of silver, and jewels of gold, and raiment: And the LORD gave the people favor in the sight of the Egyptians, so that they lent unto them [such things as they required]. And they spoiled the Egyptians" *(Exodus 12:35-36 KJV)*

5. STOP THE THIEF IN PRAYER IN THIS WATCH

Midnight is an hour spiritual thieves work. Witches, wizards, warlocks, occult powers all operate in this watch to steal the destinies of many people. Destinies are exchanged. In this watch the demonic is at its peak. Most of the negative and evil happenings in your life are orchestrated by the enemy in this watch.

If you learn to pray from 12 midnight to 3.00AM, you can stop a lot of the machinations of the evil one against your life. You will advance in the school of power if you pray a lot in this Watch.

"And she arose at midnight, and took my son from beside me, while thine handmaid slept, and laid it in

her bosom, and laid her dead child in my bosom" (1 *Kings 3:20 KJV*)

6. IT IS TIME FOR SPIRITUAL WARFARE

Pray strategic warfare prayers at this hour. You don't have to wait for the enemy to steal or bring calamity before you put him where he belongs. Come against delays and demonic strongholds in your life, city and family.

"So Gideon, and the hundred men that [were] with him, came unto the outside of the <u>camp in the beginning of the middle watch;</u> and they had but newly set the watch: and they blew the trumpets, and brake the pitchers that [were] in their hands"
(Judges 7:19 KJV)

7. RELEASE TROUBLE INTO THE CAMP OF YOUR ENEMIES

Pray and trouble all troublemakers. Any physical or spiritual gang of people against your life, ministry or family release confusion in their midst. This is a good time to handle any group of people lying about you or spreading evil rumors about you. Stop demonic conspiracy.

"In a moment shall they die, and the people shall be troubled at midnight, and pass away: and the mighty shall be taken away without hand" (Job 34:20 KJV)

8. REMOVE AND CAST DOWN SPIRITUAL GATES AND STRONGHOLDS AT MIDNIGHT

Samson wanted to deal with the gates of the philistines

but he would not until midnight. At midnight he removed the gates of the city. Gates represent power and authorities in a place. Pray and make declaration that the gates of hell will not prevail against you. If you are into ministry in a city you will need to pray and handle the spiritual gates of the city. Pray against the spiritual gates of poverty, gates of destruction and gates of death in your family. Remove the gates and cast them down, in Jesus name. In the bible days when the gates of a city were removed, that city became vulnerable. As you handle these spiritual gates, you make your enemies vulnerable.

"And Samson lay till midnight, and arose at midnight, and took the doors of the gate of the city, and the two posts, and went away with them, bar and all, and put [them] upon his shoulders, and carried them up to the top of an hill that [is] before Hebron" (Judges 16:3 KJV)

9. RELEASE WARRING ANGELS TO FIGHT FOR YOU

This is also a time to release warring angels to fight for you. It was a warring angel that was released to slay the Assyrians. Enforce strong angelic activity in your life. The angel was released in the third watch. In the verse below when the people got up in Morning watch (which is 3.00 AM to 6.00 AM.), they discovered what had been done.

The *night in* this verse refers to midnight.

"And it came to pass that night, that the angel of the LORD went out, and smote in the camp of the Assyrians an hundred fourscore and five thousand:

and when they arose early in the morning, behold, they [were] all dead corpses" (2 Kings 19:35 KJV)

10. PRAY FOR GRACE NOT TO DENY JESUS

Pray and receive grace not to deny Jesus no matter when or what. It was in this watch that Peter the apostle, denied Jesus. The cock crows at 3:00 AM according to the scriptures. Jesus told Peter *before* the cock crows, which was between 12 midnight and 3.00 AM, that he would deny Him.

"Jesus answered him, Wilt thou lay down thy life for my sake? Verily, verily, I say unto thee, The cock shall not crow, till thou hast denied me thrice"
(John 13:38 KJV)

You should also pray against denial and rejection in your life. You can pray saying, Father spare me denials in this life.

FOURTH WATCH/MORNING WATCH/DAWN WATCH 3.00 AM TO 6.00 AM

1. PRAY FOR TOTAL VICTORY OVER YOUR ENEMIES.

The Israelites got total victory over the Egyptians at the Red Sea. And this happened in the morning watch. You pray for total defeat and the end of all adversaries.

"And the Egyptians pursued, and went in after them to the midst of the sea, [even] all Pharaoh's horses, his chariots, and his horsemen. And it came to

pass, that in the morning watch the LORD looked unto the host of the Egyptians through the pillar of fire and of the cloud, and troubled the host of the Egyptians" (Exodus 14:23-24 KJV)

King Saul and the army of Israelites had total victory over the Ammonites in the morning watch. Conquer and dominate every opposition in your life in the morning watch.

"And it was [so] on the morrow, that Saul put the people in three companies; and they came into the midst of the host in the morning watch, and slew the Ammonites until the heat of the day: and it came to pass, that they which remained were scattered, so that two of them were not left together"
(1 Samuel 11:11 KJV)

Joshua and the people of Israel also got total victory over the city of Jericho in the dawning of the day which is the Morning watch. The morning watch is a good time to make confessions like "I am more than a conqueror". Supernatural victories await you in the morning watch.

"And it came to pass on the seventh day, that they rose early about the dawning of the day, and compassed the city after the same manner seven times: only on that day they compassed the city seven times" (Joshua 6:15 KJV)

2. TIME TO WALK AND OVERCOME EVERY TURBULENCE IN YOUR LIFE

Pray and handle every form of turbulence, turmoil and

confusion in your life. If there is turmoil in your marriage, in your family, in your ministry this Watch is a great time to pray and handle them. Jesus came walking over the seas in this watch. Jesus did not walk over the sea till the fourth watch. In the morning watch walk over the situations of life.

In this Watch pray for peace in nations and regions of the world where there is turmoil and wars.

"And he saw them toiling in rowing; for the wind was contrary unto them: and about <u>the fourth watch</u> of the night he cometh unto them, walking upon the sea, and would have passed by them" (Mark 6:48 KJV)

3. *PRAY AND OVERCOME YOUR FEARS*

Jesus quieted the fears of the disciples in the morning watch. In this watch pray in tongues to overcome any phobias you might have. Overcome the fear of failure, disappointment, the unexpected, death and disaster.

"And when the disciples saw him walking on the sea, they were troubled, saying, It is a spirit; and they cried out for fear. But straightway Jesus spake unto them, saying, Be of good cheer; it is I; be not afraid" (Matthew 14:26-27 KJV)

4. *RECEIVE THE SONGS OF THE SPIRIT*

This is the watch to receive great songs of the Spirit. And when you receive them sing them until the anointing is stirred up inside because the songs of the spirit are your victory songs. If you are very sensitive you have probably realized that most of the time when you get up in the morning, there is a particular song on your heart. These are songs of the spirit released to you by the morning stars.

Spend time and worship in this watch.

If you are a music minister, you can get a lot of new and fresh songs from heaven if you observe this watch. You can be a great song writer if you will get up in this watch.

"When the morning stars sang together, and all the sons of God shouted for joy? (Job 38:7 KJV).

Who are the Morning stars? The morning stars are a class of angels. Most of the time in the bible, angels are referred to as stars. For example, when the devil fell from heaven, the scriptures declare that his tail drew a third of the stars of heaven. The stars refer to angels. So, they fell with a third of the angels of heaven. They are now what is known as fallen angels. They are different from demons.

"And there appeared another wonder in heaven; and behold a great red dragon, having seven heads and ten horns, and seven crowns upon his heads. And his tail drew <u>the third part of the stars of heaven,</u> and did cast them to the earth: and the dragon stood before the woman which was ready to be delivered, for to devour her child as soon as it was born"
(Revelation 12:3-4 KJV)

5. *COMMAND YOUR MORNING AND LET THE DAWN KNOW ITS PLACE*

This is the watch to program your day. It is time to program your destiny with your tongue using Words of power. Make declaration and decrees concerning your life, ministry, business, family, children, nation and virtually whatever you are involved in. *"Hast thou commanded the morning since thy days; [and] caused the dayspring to know his place" (Job 38:12 KJV).*

What does it mean to command your morning? It simply means to impregnate your morning. Don't be surprised. The morning has a womb so it can be impregnated. *"Thy people [shall be] willing in the day of thy power, in the beauties of holiness from the womb of the morning: thou hast the dew of thy youth" (Psalms 110:3 KJV)*

The morning has a womb and you can impregnate it with a seed. Which seed are we talking about? The seed of the Word. Because the word is a seed. *"Now the parable is this: The seed is the word of God" (Luke 8:11 KJV).*

Make confessions. Speak scriptures like, "I am the head and not the tail. I am more than a conqueror. I have overcome today. I walk in prosperity, favor and health today. I am sustained with blessing and honor. I walk in power. I walk in miracles." As you talk like this in the Morning watch, you are impregnating and commanding your morning.

Seize the dawn and let your day know its place. Tell your day, "this is the day the Lord has made I will rejoice and be glad in you. Hey day, you were made for my rejoicing.

Hallelujah." Let your day know its place before it messes up.

6. *YEARN AND LONG FOR GOD*

The Morning watch is a good time to yearn and long for the sweet fellowship of the Holy Spirit. It is a great time to enjoy the presence of God.

It is also a great time to build up an expectation of God's miracles in your life.

"My soul [waiteth] for the Lord more than they that watch for the morning: [I say, more than] they that watch for the morning" (Psalms 130:6 KJV)

7. *RECEIVE GOD'S MERCIES AND COMPASSION*

In the morning receive the mercies, the compassion and the lovingkindness of God. They are renewed and released every morning. Meditate and relish in the compassion of God.

"[It is of] the LORD'S mercies that we are not consumed, because his compassions fail not. [They are] new every morning: great [is] thy faithfulness" (Lamentations 3:22-23 KJV)

"To shew forth thy lovingkindness in the morning, and thy faithfulness every night" (Psalms 92:2 KJV)

8. *EXPECT TO HEAR THE VOICE OF GOD*

The morning watch is a great time to be still and hear the voice of God. Expect to hear the *Now* word of God for your life and concerning issues facing you. Receive divine direction and instructions from God. Get a quiet place and hear what He will tell you.

"I was up before sunrise, crying for help, hoping for a word from you" (Psalms 119:147 MSG)

9. *PRAY AGAINST WORRYING AND TAKE CONTROL OF YOUR MIND.*

This is the time the evil one sends thoughts of worry to many people. Most people get up and worry at dawn on their beds. You should pray and attack any thoughts of worry shot against you from the devil. Pray against anxiety. Uproot any seeds of worry, doubt, anxiety and unbelief sown in your heart.

"When I lie down, I say, When shall I arise, and the night be gone? and I am full of tossings to and fro unto the dawning of the day" (Job 7:4 KJV).

GROUP WATCHING

As individuals it can be very difficult to observe all the watches in one night because of your work schedule and other activities. So, there is what is called Group Watching.

Group Watching is when a group of people decide and plan to observe the watches. They appoint a person or persons who will observe the watch convenient to them.

Nehemiah and his men practiced group watching—everyone in their own chosen watch and in their houses.

"And I said unto them, Let not the gates of Jerusalem be opened until the sun be hot; and while they stand by, let them shut the doors, and bar [them]: and appoint watches of the inhabitants of Jerusalem, every one in his watch, and every one [to be] over against his house" (Nehemiah 7:3 KJV)

The priests too in Judah also practiced Group Watching

"But let none come into the house of the LORD, save the priests, and they that minister of the Levites; they shall go in, for they [are] holy: but all the people shall keep the watch of the LORD" (2 Chronicles 23:6 KJV)

At times when you need a miracle or a turnaround as a family, a ministry, a city or even a nation, you can come into agreement and practice Group Watching. Some people pray in the First watch. Another group in the second, another in the third and another in the fourth watch. The benefits and blessings that are released in group watching is for the collective.

Make sure you get serious and trusted people who will not sleep in their watches. Jesus had people who could not watch with Him. They slept on their watch. *"And he cometh unto the disciples, and findeth them asleep, and saith unto Peter, What, could ye not watch with me one hour? Watch and pray, that ye enter not into temptation: the spirit indeed [is] willing, but the flesh [is] weak" (Matthew 26:40-41 KJV)*

Churches and ministries can practice this. Family and friends can also practice group watching.

CHAPTER 7

HOURS OF THE DAY

We discovered earlier in this book that the 24-hour day has two divisions— Day and Night. We have discussed the prayers you need to pray in the night watches, the general ones and the specific. Now we want to put our attention on the Day.

Traditionally, the 24-hour day has been divided into eight watches, four in the day and four in the night. But you will rarely find that the day was divided into watches in the bible. You don't find a watch of the day. Almost all the time you find a watch, it is of the night. So, what about the day? In the scriptures, the junctions of time in the day are called HOURS OF THE DAY. It was Jesus who revealed this to us in the gospel of John.

"Jesus answered, Are there not twelve <u>hours in the day</u>? If any man walk in the day, he stumbleth not, because he seeth the light of this world" (John 11:9 KJV)

Jesus said there are 12-hours in the day. So in the day, we have *Hours* as the Junctions and not *watches*. See these from scriptures:

1. *"For these are not drunken, as ye suppose, seeing it is [but] <u>the third hour of the day</u>" (Acts 2:15 KJV)*

Here we see the third hour of the day.

2. *"He saw in a vision evidently about <u>the ninth</u> <u>hour of the day</u> an angel of God coming in to him, and saying unto him, Cornelius" (Acts 10:3 KJV)*

Over here we see the ninth hour of the day.

You never find the fifth watch, sixth watch, seventh watch or eighth watch in the scriptures.

THE 12-HOURS OF THE DAY

7.00 AM- First hour of the day.
8.00 AM- Second hour of the day.
9.00 AM- Third hour of the day
10.00 AM-Fourth hour of the day
11.00 AM-Fifth hour of the day
12.00 NOON-Sixth hour of the day
1.00 PM-Seventh hour of the day
2.00 PM-Eighth hour of the day
3.00 PM-Ninth hour of the day
4.00 PM-Tenth hour of the day
5.00 PM- Eleventh hour of the day
6.00 PM- Twelfth hour of the day

You must understand why the first hour of the day is 7:00 AM and not 6:00 AM. We are dealing with completed hours. So, the first completed hour of the day is 7:00 AM. Actually, an hour is a span. The first hour starts from 6:00 AM and ends at 7:00 AM. The second starts from 7:01 AM and ends at 8:00 AM. And it continues like that.

GENERAL PRAYERS AND ACTIVITIES FOR ALL THE HOURS OF THE DAY

Now there are certain prayers and spiritual activities you can do for all the hours of the day. You can pray them at any hour of the day.

1. Pray against arrows that fly by day.

"Thou shalt not be afraid for the terror by night; [nor] for the arrow [that] flieth by day" (Psalms 91:5 KJV)

In the day pray and come against demonic arrows shot against you and your destiny. It can be an arrow of sickness, disgrace, death, doubt. It can be against your ministry, marriage, finance, children and family. Stop the arrow and return it to the sender. We have already discovered that terrors are by the night and arrows fly in the day.

2. Pray against the drought of the day.

"[Thus] I was; in the day the drought consumed me, and the frost by night; and my sleep departed from mine eyes" (Genesis 31:40 KJV)

Handle the spiritual drought in your finances, your joy, your peace that the devil sends during the day. The frost is by the night but the drought is by the day. Prophetically, all these are spiritual elements used against you by the evil one. In the day pray against them.

Also pray for cities and nations around the world to stop the attacks of famine and drought In Jesus mighty name.

3. Be conscious of the Pillar of cloud going with you.

"And the LORD will create upon every dwelling place of mount Zion, and upon her assemblies, a cloud and smoke by day, and the shining of a flaming fire by night: for upon all the glory [shall be] a defence" **(Isaiah 4:5 KJV)**

Walk in the consciousness that there is a pillar of cloud going with you during the day. When you are born again you dwell in Zion. And in Zion God creates upon all the dwelling places a cloud by day. And you are the dwelling place of God if you are born again. God went ahead of the Israelites as the pillar of cloud by day. Know that God goes ahead of you as you leave your house. God leads you.

"And the LORD went before them by day in a pillar of a cloud, to lead them the way; and by night in a pillar of fire, to give them light; to go by day and night" **(Exodus 13:21 KJV)**

Never say you are alone. If you are born again it is too late to be alone. God has become your defense.

4. Pray that the sun will not smite you by day.

"The sun shall not smite thee by day, nor the moon by night" **(Psalms 121:6 KJV)**

You have to pray and stop the sun smiting you by day. This is how David prayed. He was not just talking about the scorching heat of the sun. He was speaking prophetically here. The enemy can project things against you by the sun and the moon and you want to stop them.

CHAPTER 8

SPECIFIC PRAYERS TO PRAY AT SPECIFIC HOURS OF THE DAY

Now we get into the specific hours of the day and the prayers and spiritual activities that must be prayed. We will discuss the hours of the day revealed to us in the scriptures.

THIRD HOUR OF THE DAY- 9.00 AM

1. PRAY AGAINST IDLENESS AND RECEIVE DIVINE APPOINTMENT

This is the hour to pray against idleness and joblessness. Pray for your divine appointments and employment. Pray for productivity in your business, marriage, ministry and life. If you are believing God for employment this is a good time to pray. Curse every spirit of joblessness. Curse every spirit of laziness and lethargy that stops you from doing what you have to do.

"And he went out about the third hour, and saw others standing idle in the marketplace" (Matthew 20:3 KJV)

2. MEDITATE ON THE CRUCIFIXION OF THE LORD JESUS CHRIST

"And it was the third hour, and they crucified him" (Mark 15:25 KJV)

In this hour meditate and brood on the crucifixion of the Lord Jesus Christ. Think about His love for you.

Meditate on the fact that your sins are forgiven you. Be grateful and thank Him for what He did for you on the cross. Think about the riches of His redemption.

When you are meditating on the crucifixion, don't just see Jesus hanging on the cross. Think like Paul, the apostle and say, *"I am crucified with Christ: nevertheless I live; yet not I, but Christ liveth in me: and the life which I now live in the flesh I live by the faith of the Son of God, who loved me, and gave himself for me" (Galatians 2:20 KJV).*

Speak to yourself that the old you have been crucified with Jesus on the cross. The powerless, sinful and ordinary you have been crucified on the cross. You are alive, living by the faith of the son of God, Jesus.

Meditate on scriptures like this one: *"Knowing this, that our old man is crucified with [him], that the body of sin might be destroyed, that henceforth we should not serve sin" (Romans 6:6 KJV).* You will receive spiritual strength as you do this.

3. BE BEING FILLED WITH THE HOLY SPIRIT.

"For these are not drunken, as ye suppose, seeing it is [but] the third hour of the day" (Acts 2:15 KJV)

This is the hour where you fellowship with the Holy Spirit. Get filled and filled again with the Spirit of God till you are intoxicated. Get drunk with the wine of the Spirit as Paul, the apostle admonishes. *"And be not drunk with wine, wherein is excess; but be filled with the Spirit"*

(Ephesians 5:18 KJV).

This is a really great time to speak in the language of the Spirit because the first tongues in the church of the Living God were spoken in the third hour of the day. You might find time on your job, or while driving to get a few minutes and speak in tongues. You can rush to the washroom and speak in tongues. Hallelujah!

There are things you can do to get filled with the Holy Spirit and stir up the well of anointing of God in you.

"Speaking to yourselves in psalms and hymns and spiritual songs, singing and making melody in your heart to the Lord" (Ephesians 5:19 KJV)

Speak to yourself. All by yourself speak the Psalms to yourself. Sing songs of the Spirit. Make confession declaring that you are anointed. As you do that you will get drunk with the Wine of the Spirit.

4. PRAY FOR ALCOHOLICS AND DRUNKARDS

Pray for all drunkards across the world that they be set free from the bondage of alcoholism. **"For these are not drunken, as ye suppose, seeing it is [but] the third hour of the day" (Acts 2:15 KJV)**

SIXTH HOUR OF THE DAY – 12 NOON

1. TIME TO CRY ALOUD IN PRAYER

"Evening, and morning, and at noon, will I pray, and cry aloud: and he shall hear my voice" (Psalms 55:17 KJV)

At the sixth hour you cry aloud in prayer. This is referring to a cry of the heart. If your time will allow spend some quality time in prayer during this hour.

2. PRAY AND CANCEL DESTRUCTION SENT AGAINST YOU.

"[Nor] for the pestilence [that] walketh in darkness; [nor] for the destruction [that] wasteth at noonday" (Psalms 91:6 KJV)

The enemy sends destruction at noonday. So, pray against any form of destruction prepared and organized against your ministry, finances, family, education, city or country. Stop any form of waste in life in this hour. Declare that your destiny will not be wasted. Your resources will not be wasted.

3. PRAY FOR GOD WHO IS YOUR SHEPHERD TO GIVE YOU ALL AROUND REST

"Tell me, O thou whom my soul loveth, where thou feedest, where thou makest [thy flock] to rest at noon: for why should I be as one that turneth aside by the flocks of thy companions? (Songs of Solomon 1:7 KJV)

At noon pray to have rest in your life. There are some people who are always struggling from one battle to another, from one defeat to another. Receive the rest of God at noon. The scripture declares that we are the sheep of his pasture and He is our Shepherd. *"Know ye that the LORD he [is] God: [it is] he [that] hath made us, and not we ourselves; [we are] his people, and the sheep of his pasture" (Psalms 100:3 KJV)*

"The LORD [is] my shepherd; I shall not want" (Psalms 23:1 KJV).

God has a place of rest for you. Pray and say, 'Oh God show me where you make your sheep to rest. Make declarations like: "My family knows the rest of God; My marriage enjoys the rest of God. My body knows the rest of God". All at noon.

4. PRAY AGAINST IDLENESS AND RECEIVE DIVINE APPOINTMENT

It is also the hour to pray against idleness and joblessness. Pray for your divine appointments and employment. Pray for productivity in your business, marriage, ministry and life. If you are believing God for employment this is a good time to pray. Curse every spirit of joblessness. Curse every spirit of laziness and lethargy that stops you from doing what you have to do.

"Again he went out about the sixth and ninth hour, and did likewise" (Matthew 20:5 KJV)

5. PRAY AND COME AGAINST EVERY ATTACK OF DARKNESS

"Now from the sixth hour there was darkness over all the land unto the ninth hour" (Matthew 27:45 KJV)

Jesus was crucified at about 9:00 AM. At the sixth hour darkness covered the whole land. The darkness waited till noon to cover the land. At noon pray and cause the light of God to scatter every darkness sent into your life from the camp of the enemy. Pray and stop the activities of the kingdom of darkness.

6. PRAY AGAINST WEARINESS IN YOUR JOURNEY OF LIFE AND RECEIVE THE STRENGTH OF GOD

"Now Jacob's well was there. Jesus therefore, being wearied with [his] journey, sat thus on the well: [and] it was about the sixth hour" (John 4:6 KJV).

At the sixth hour ask God to strengthen you for the journey of life. Receive strength for your life's mandate and assignment. At times in your Christian journey you get tired and weary. You must be energized at this hour.

You should also pray against physical tiredness and stress. Receive strength to complete your assignment and achieve your goals.

7. SPEND TIME TO PRAY APOSTOLIC PRAYERS

"On the morrow, as they went on their journey, and drew nigh unto the city, Peter went up upon the housetop to pray about the sixth hour" (Acts 10:9 KJV)

Pray apostolic prayers to affect nations, cities, families and destinies. It was at this hour that Peter, the apostle went to pray and in prayer he was directed to visit the home of Cornelius, the centurion. It was because of this prayer session that the first gentile family was converted and saved. Change nations and destinies in prayer at this hour. Make apostolic declarations at this hour.

8. RECEIVE OPEN HEAVENS AND VISIONS AT MIDDAY

"At midday, O king, I saw in the way a light from heaven, above the brightness of the sun, shining round about me and them which journeyed with me"
(Acts 26:13 KJV).

Pray the heavens to open over you, your family and everything you do. Yield yourself to visions at this hour. Pray and receive the Light of God's countenance at noon.

"[There be] many that say, Who will shew us [any] good? LORD, lift thou up the light of thy countenance upon us" (Psalms 4:6 KJV)

9. AT MIDDAY MOCK YOUR ENEMIES IN PRAYER

"And it came to pass at noon, that Elijah mocked them, and said, Cry aloud: for he [is] a god; either he is talking, or he is pursuing, or he is in a journey, [or] peradventure he sleepeth, and must be awaked"
(1 Kings 18:27 KJV)

Pray and in prayer mock your enemies with the word of God. Tell the devil he is a liar. The scriptures declare, Jesus made a spectacle of principalities and powers. *"And having disarmed the powers and authorities, he made a public spectacle of them, triumphing over them by the cross" (Colossians 2:15 NIV).*

At noon remind the devil that Jesus conquered him already. And very soon he will be arrested and thrown into the bottomless pit. Let every devil know you are seated far above in heavenly places. Declare that you are hidden in a rock which is Christ. And that you very safe in Christ.

You mock the devil with scriptures.

NINTH HOUR OF THE DAY- 3:00 PM

1. THE NINTH HOUR IS THE HOUR OF PRAYER

"Now Peter and John went up together into the temple <u>at the hour of prayer, [being] the ninth [hour]</u>" (Acts 3:1 KJV)

The ninth hour is one of the most important hours in the day. The scripture expressly declares it is the hour of prayer. The Apostles observed this hour of prayer. Peter and John were on their way to pray at 3:00 PM. If your schedule allows spend time in prayer at 3:00 PM. If your schedule will not allow, speak in tongues wherever you are.

2. HOUR OF MIRACLES

The ninth hour is also the hour of miracles. The first miracle recorded by the new testament church happened at the ninth hour.

"Now Peter and John went up together into the temple at the hour of prayer, [being] the ninth [hour]. And a certain man lame from his mother's womb was carried, whom they laid daily at the gate of the temple which is called Beautiful, to ask alms of them that entered into the temple; Who seeing Peter and John about to go into the temple asked an alms. And Peter, fastening his eyes upon him with John, said, Look on us. And he gave heed unto them, expecting to receive something of them. Then Peter said, Silver and gold have I none; but such as I have give I thee: In the name of Jesus Christ of Nazareth rise up and walk. And he took him by the right hand, and lifted [him] up: and immediately his feet and ankle bones received strength. And he leaping up stood, and walked, and entered with them into the temple, walking, and leaping, and praising God" (Acts 3:1-8 KJV)

At this hour receive miracles from God. Also, receive strength for anything the devil has crippled and has left lame in your life. The lame man received strength.

3. EVERY FORM OF DARKNESS IN YOUR LIFE MUST CEASE

"Now from the sixth hour there was darkness over all the land unto the ninth hour. And about the ninth hour Jesus cried with a loud voice, saying, Eli, Eli, lama" (Mathew 27:45-46 KJV)

Demand that every form of darkness in your life must come to a halt. Every form of disgrace, shame, failure, confusion must cease. Darkness in your city and nation should cease. Enforce this In Jesus name.

4. CRY OUT AGAINST LONELINESS AND REJECTION

"And about the ninth hour Jesus cried with a loud voice, saying, Eli, Eli, lama sabachthani? that is to say, My God, my God, why hast thou forsaken me? (Matthew 27:46 KJV)

Cry out against every spirit of rejection and loneliness. Your spouse can't reject you. Receive your life's companion at this hour. You cannot be forsaken.

5. TAKE COMMUNION AND HARNESS THE BENEFITS OF THE DEATH OF CHRIST

"Jesus, when he had cried again with a loud voice, yielded up the ghost" (Matthew 27:50 KJV)

Jesus actually died at exactly 3:00 PM. One of the most important events in this universe took place at this hour. I believe there is a very great and huge portal into the realm of the spirit at this hour.

Take the Lord's Supper and fellowship with the Blood and body of Christ. Do this in remembrance of the Lord.

6. PRAY FOR ALL UNSAVED SOULS

"Jesus, when he had cried again with a loud voice, yielded up the ghost" (Matthew 27:50 KJV)

This is the hour Jesus died to save the whole world. Pray for unbelievers so that they will be saved. This is because Jesus died for all men. *"And [that] he died for all, that they which live should not henceforth live unto themselves, but unto him which died for them, and rose again" (2 Corinthians 5:15 KJV)*

Pray for missions and missionaries around the world. Also pray for all persecuted Christians across the globe.

7. PRAY HISTORY CHANGING PRAYERS

"Jesus, when he had cried again with a loud voice, yielded up the ghost" (Matthew 27:50 KJV)

The history of the world was changed for good in this hour by the death of Jesus. Pray that God makes you a history maker, a pathfinder, a pacesetter and a trailblazer like Jesus.

8. HOUR OF VISIONS

"He saw in a vision evidently about the ninth hour of the day an angel of God coming in to him, and

saying unto him, Cornelius" (Acts 10:3 KJV)

"And Cornelius said, Four days ago I was fasting until this hour; and at the ninth hour I prayed in my house, and, behold, a man stood before me in bright clothing" (Acts 10:30 KJV)

Ask the Holy spirit to give you visions of your future. Call unto Him and He will show you great and mighty things you do not know. And when the Holy Spirit shows you visions, write them down and run with them.

9. TIME OF THE EVENING SACRIFICE WITH OPEN HEAVENS

"And it came to pass, when midday was past, and they <u>prophesied until the [time] of the offering of the [evening] sacrifice,</u> that [there was] neither voice, nor any to answer, nor any that regarded"
(1 Kings 18:29 KJV)

I believe you have heard the story of Prophet Elijah and the Prophets of Baal. Each prophet was to call on their God to send down fire and the God that answered by fire would be the true God. Elijah allowed the prophets of Baal to prophesy past midday until the time of the evening sacrifice. The moment it was time for the evening sacrifice Prophet Elijah jumped to the scene and said it was his turn to prophesy. Elijah knew that at the time of the Evening sacrifice the heavens are opened and when he called down fire it would come with ease. *"And it came to pass <u>at</u> [the time of] the offering of the [evening] sacrifice, that Elijah the prophet came near, and said, LORD God of Abraham, Isaac, and of Israel, let it be known* *this day that thou [art] God in Israel, and [that] I [am] thy servant, and [that] I have done all these things at thy word" (1 Kings 18:36 KJV)*

According to Josephus, the historian, the evening sacrifice was prepared around 2:30 PM and was offered between 3:00-3:30 PM. This is the reason why Jesus was offered up at 3:00 PM, because typologically, Jesus is our evening sacrifice.

At this hour pray and demand open heavens over your life and all you are involved in. It is a time for great manifestation.

10. HOUR OF ANGELIC VISITATIONS

"While I was still in prayer, Gabriel, the man I had seen in the earlier vision, came to me in swift flight about the time of the evening sacrifice"
(Daniel 9:21 KJV)

It is the time to receive angelic visitations and encounters. Daniel received angelic visitation at the time of the evening sacrifice which is the ninth hour.
Pray for insight and understanding at this hour

11. PRAY AGAINST IDLENESS AND RECEIVE DIVINE APPOINTMENT

It is also the hour to pray against idleness and joblessness. Pray for your divine appointments and employment. Pray for productivity in your business, marriage, ministry and life. If you are believing God for employment this is a good time to pray. Curse every spirit of joblessness. Curse every spirit of laziness and lethargy that stops you from doing what you have to do.

"Again he went out about the sixth and ninth hour, and did likewise" (Matthew 20:5 KJV)

12. HOUR OF DELIVERY

Pray travailing prayers now. Nine is the number for delivery. Travail and give birth to every vision and idea you are pregnant with.

"Who hath heard such a thing? who hath seen such things? Shall the earth be made to bring forth in one day? [or] shall a nation be born at once? for as soon as Zion travailed, she brought forth her children"
(Isaiah 66:8 KJV)

ELEVENTH HOUR OF THE DAY-5:00 PM

1. PRAY AGAINST IDLENESS AND RECEIVE DIVINE APPOINTMENT

This is also the hour to pray against idleness and joblessness. Pray for your divine appointments and employment. Pray for productivity in your business, marriage, ministry and life. If you are believing God for employment this is a good time to pray. Curse every spirit of joblessness. Curse every spirit of laziness and lethargy that stops you from doing what you have to do.

"And about the eleventh hour he went out, and found others standing idle, and saith unto them, Why stand ye here all the day idle?(Matthew 20:6 KJV)

2. PRAY FOR UNCOMMON FAVOR

"And when they came that [were hired] about the eleventh hour, they received every man a penny. But when the first came, they supposed that they should have received more; and they likewise received every man a penny" (Matthew 20:9-10 KJV)

Pray for uncommon favor in this hour. Ask God to give you what naturally you cannot obtain by your strength. Those who were hired at the last eleventh hour got favored. Ask God to magnify your efforts.

Also pray against jealousy in this hour. All the others employed earlier were jealous of those who were favored & hired in the eleventh hour.

WHICH TIMEZONE TO PRAY

Since there are different time zones in the world, which time zone do use to observe the watches or which junctions do you use? For example, when is 9.00 AM in the United States of America, it will be about 10.00 PM in China. So, when is the third hour of the day in the united states, it will be the second watch of the night in China. If I am an American and I travel to China for a conference, which time zone do I use to observe the watches or which junction of time do I pray?

Or for example, when is 1.00 AM in Ghana, West Africa, it will be about 8.00 PM in the United States. This means whilst it is third watch in Ghana, it is only the first watch in United States. What do I do? Do you pray the prayers for the two separate time zones?

It is quite simple. The time zone is ruled by the Sun by day and the moon by night as explained earlier on this book. God gave the Sun to rule the day and the moon and the stars to rule the night.

"The sun to rule by day: for his mercy [endureth] for ever: The moon and stars to rule by night: for his mercy [endureth] for ever" (Psalms 136:8-9 KJV)

When you find yourself in a such a situation where you travel to a different time zone or have family and connections living in another time zone, you just have to pray using the time zone you are present in.

You must understand that if witches and wizards plan something against you in another time zone, in other to affect you it must submit to the governance of the sun, moon and stars in your time zone. In the same way the Chinese government if it wants to meet the American government for a meeting in America, must operate in the time zone of America and vice-versa, any demonic operation in another time zone must submit and obtain permission from the ruling authorities in that specific time zone.

So, what you need to do is just pray using the time zone you find yourself in at any particular point in time. The Time-Portal created in each time zone is connected to the governance of the sun, moon and stars. It is connected to whether it is Day or Night at a particular place.

BENEFITS OF PRAYING AT THE JUNCTIONS OF TIME

1. Praying at the junctions of time allows you to take advantage of the spiritual activities at the portals of time. You have ease of access to certain spiritual blessings and encounters. The heightened spiritual activity enables and enhances prayer. This is because in prayer you are engaging the spiritual energy of God.

2. Praying at the junctions of time makes you cover a lot of prayer topics. There are certain prayer topics you might never pray about, but as you routinely practice this, you get to pray them.

3. Praying at the junctions of time helps you pray around the clock fulfilling the admonishment of scripture to pray without ceasing. *"Pray without ceasing" (1 Thessalonians 5:17 KJV)*

4. Observing the watches is one of the kinds of prayer Paul the apostle entreats us to pray. *"And pray in the Spirit on all occasions with <u>all kinds of prayers</u> and requests. With this in mind, be alert and always keep on praying for all the saints" (Ephesians 6:18 KJV)*

Friend, a great tool of prayer has been handed over to you in this book. Put it to use and it will cause you to reign and be master of all circumstances. You are born again to reign again. Establish the kingdom of God in your world.

ABOUT THE AUTHOR

Dr. Mark K. Amoateng, is the founder and Senior Pastor of Christ Palace International Ministries and President of Mark Amoateng Ministries. He is a unique and vibrant minister of God for these present times. He ministers under the divine influence of the Holy Spirit and strong insight in the Word of God. Dr. Mark is an awesome teacher of the Word of God. His messages are so profound and yet have a touch of simplicity. Pastor Mark's faith is contagious and affects those who come into contact with him. He picks the Word of God and holds it as it is. His operation in the prophetic, combined with his faith and insight in the Word of God, makes his impact strong, effective and long lasting. Give him a little attention and the divine verities of the Word of God become real to you. Pastor Mark is a medical doctor by training but now pursues the high calling of God on his life fulltime. He is happily married to Lady Pastor Magdelene Doris Amoateng also a medical doctor by profession. Their marriage is graciously blessed with two children, Amethyst and Johanan. Together, they fulfill the glorious divine mandate on their lives. He lives in Houston, Texas with his family. He is the author of a few titles including How to receive from God and The Wonders of Speaking in tongues. He also authors the highly anointed daily devotionals called The Voice Devotional.

Made in the USA
Middletown, DE
10 July 2020